CUSTOMIZED FOAMS

Deconstruction & Reconstruction

BY ANTHONY BOYD

Copyright 2017

Anaghe Inc.

All rights reserved. Written permission must be secured from the publisher to use or reproduce any part of this book, except for brief quotations in critical reviews or articles.

WWW.ANAGHE.COM

https://www.youtube.com/user/AnagheInc

YOUR MEMBERSHIP AT WWW.ANAGHE.COM IS FREE WITH THE PURCHASE OF THIS BOOK TO REDEEM YOUR MEMBERSHIP & WATCH THE INSTRUCTIONAL VIDEOS PLEASE FOLLOW THE STEPS BELOW.

BOOK BUYERS: SIGN UP ON THE WEBSITE AND FORWARD PROOF OF PURCHASE (RECEIPT WITH CONFIRMATION #) AN APPROVAL NOTIFACATION WILL BE

SENT BY EMAIL WITH IN 24 HRS.

NEW MEMBERS: MAKE MEMBERSHIP PAYMENT FOR EBOOK DOWNLOAD & VIDEO ACCESS THEN SIGN UP ON THE SITE FOR YOUR APPROVAL NOTIFACATION ALLOW UP TO 24 HRS FOR PROCESSING.

Contents

INTRODUCTION 6

GRIP REMOVAL..8

BREAKDOWN..11

LINER BREAKDOWN..14

PATTERN CREATION 17

RECONSTRUCTION PREP 24

SNEAKER RECONSTRUCTION..................................29

GRIP BACK ON 43

STITCH CLASSIFACTION & INSTRUCTION 47

REVERSE OXIDATION PROCESS 49

REFLECTIVE BOX AND LIGHT 50

APPLY WHITENER 51

WRAP SHOES 52

Introduction

It was the beginning of the summer in Buffalo NY the Fruit Belt was full of kids excited about the possibilities the vacation would offer. Often we would gather at a local corner store on Carlton to play video games after eating cold lunches at the CAO Center. But this one particular day would be forever sketched in my mind. I had a covatus haircut, royal blue terrycloth short set the tank top had a white and red stripe across the chest area with matching knee socks lol. And get this a fresh pair of Jointz from Hills, they was white with gold trim, all leather and yes the brand name was The Jointz lol. Now I had kept being asked if I had heard it yet I would say no then this day happen to my life. I step out the store and Boo had it banging out his radio that song changed my life the little amount he allowed me to hear before he start complaining about his batteries. I walked away so inspired saying to myself as well as asking God " No matter what ever happens in my life make it so that I forever have something to do with Hip Hop ". Never would I have ever imagined that the skills that I acquired through this Art form would carry me to this point in my life. This space of sharing what it shared with me. This

ANAGHE INC.

Book is here by dedicated to that Song and the Composers of it.

Grip Removal

In Order to remove the grip you'll need the following tools. An electric stove or Gas stove, 2 Pots one large one small a Strainer that fits your large pot. A glass jar and dropper a butter knife and lastly Nail Polish remover with 50 to 100% Acetone.

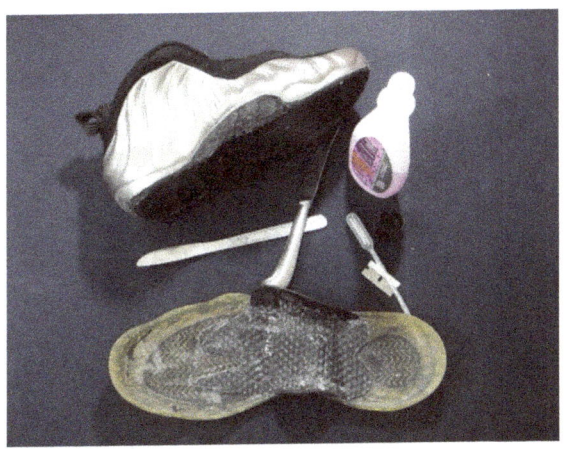

Remove the insole and begin to score the sneaker with a butter knife all the way around where the grip meets the upper. Use the dropper to exact the nail polish and apply it to the scored areas all the way around. Mix a half of bottle of nail polish with water in your small pot and bring it to a boil please be aware that it may sizzle when doing so. Your mixing these for the following reasons:

1. To dilute it because the polish is highly flammable so be careful when working over a gas stove we recommend using an electric plug in eye as shown no flame no fire.
2. This combination will be our solvent for the inside of the sneaker. Hot acetone water.

Bring your large pot of water to a boil and place your strainer in it now place the sneakers on top of the strainer and pour the solvent solution inside the sneaker high enough to cover the surface should be no higher than ½" reason being the material will begin to absorb the solvent and it make leak threw. Use the strainer to move the solvent around to ensure the solution reaches down inside the sneaker completely around. Pour out the solvent after it cools then place the sneaker back on the pot without the strainer allowing the steam heat to penetrate the scored and solvent areas for 30 to 60 mins. Remove them and begin to check for lose portions of grip around the upper use the dropper to apply more NP remover to these lose areas. Once applied use a butter knife to pry the grip away from the upper. Working from the front to the back if it feels like your using too much force to separate the grip from the upper apply more NPR to that area only. Place them back on the pot of boiling water and repeat the entire process till the grips are completely removed.

Breakdown

Only tools needed here is a fresh Razor Blade a seam ripper and pen to name and mark the pieces left or right, lace holes, upper, inside and outside ankle cushion, piping, interfacing etc.

Begin by removing the pull tab in the back then start on the outside portion of the lace holes run the razor all the way around till all the stitches are cut.

Now turn the inside ankle cushion on the other side by pulling it free from the sneakers so it's on the outside of the upper and the seams are showing. Run your razor over the seams till it is removed from the upper. Go back to the lace holes but this time we'll be doing the inside portion. Frist we need to remove the piping by cutting it in half, use the razor once more and run it over the top of it till it splits. Then re-run the razor under the lace holes to rip the stitches for it and the piping. Now pull the outside ankle cushion away from the upper and run the razor around the bottom of it till it's completely free.

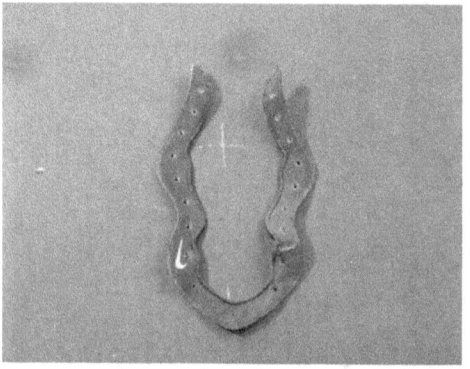

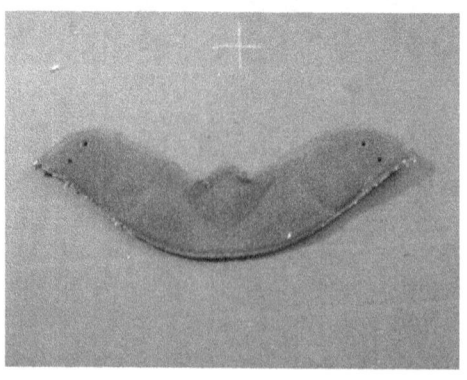

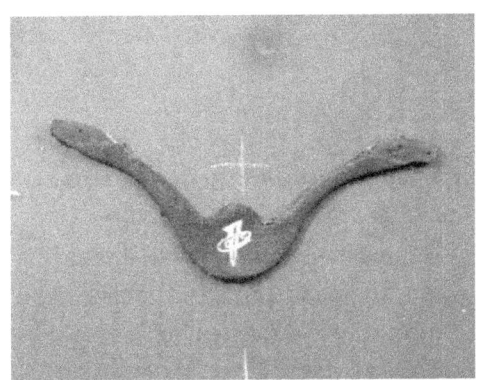

Liner Breakdown

Remove the tongue tabs and grosgrain pull tabs and then begin to rip the stitches on the Spacer Fabric with a razor. You may have to really pull to separate it from the nylon, try loosening a few stitches and pull gently. One option when dealing with these heavy glued areas is to apply the water and NPR.

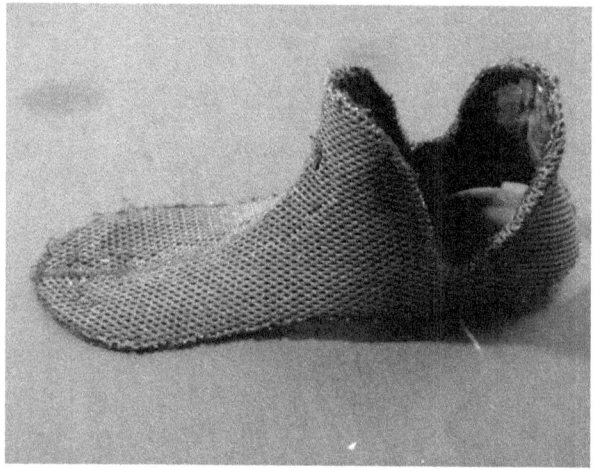

When you reach the bottom of the heel area it will be necessary to cut your spacer fabric free at the heel area only.

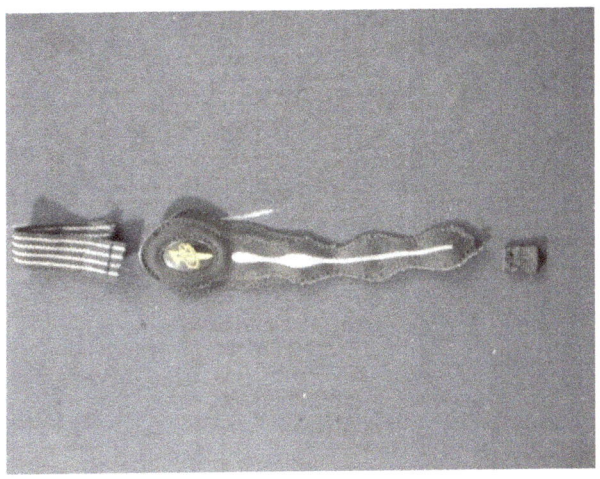

Pull gently and cut as close as you can get to the bottom. Afterward check to see how much fabric was left to give yourself an estimate of how much more to add when making adjustments on your final patterns. Clean them of any loose stitches and remove the zig zag stitch down the front and back of the spacer fabric. One side will be used to create patterns for the new spacer fabric and inside liner this is the lyrca material the spacer fabric was attached to and still attached to the sneaker itself. We will discuss in depth how to cut and reattach the liner in the Sneaker Reconstruction chapter.

CUSTOMIZED FOAMS

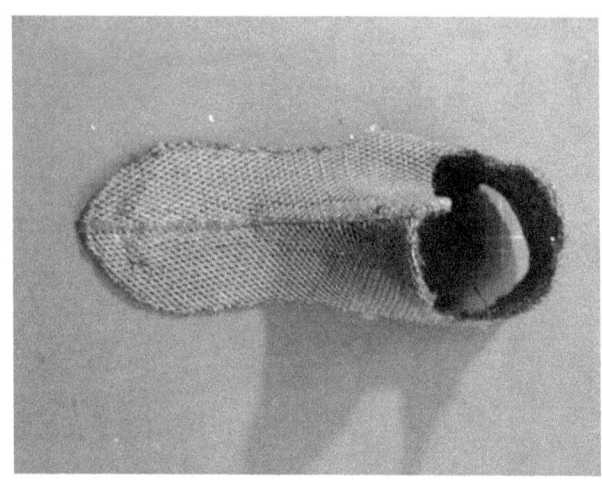

ANAGHE INC.

Pattern Creation

This is where we create patterns to replace the tongue tabs the lace holes the inside and outside ankle cushions the inner and outer liner and the upper. The tools needed to complete the task are the following:

TOOLS: Pattern Paper, Rulers & Curves, Clear Plastic, Adhesive Spray and Marker

Here we will be creating patterns to replace the ones we took off the uppers these patterns will reflect any changes you made to your designs. Please keep in mind that your designs are only as good as the patterns that created them. Be sure to pick the best pieces to trace avoid stretched out pieces if possible if you have to use one compare to the others the make adjustments in that area after you trace it out. Be precise with your measurements stay close to the edge when tracing and always double check your numbers when drafting. Pattern drafting of any kind is an Art and takes years to master the process of giving a flat surface dimension. So thought out this chapter I am going to discuss certain dos and things to avoid doing as well as present a few short cuts.

CUSTOMIZED FOAMS

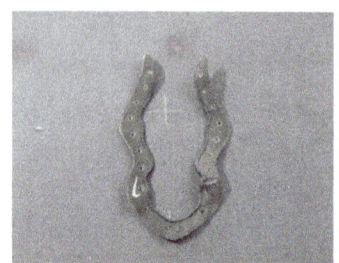

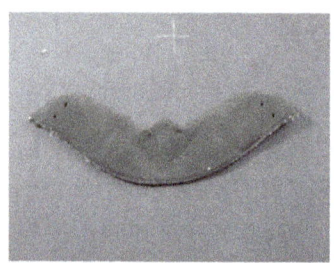

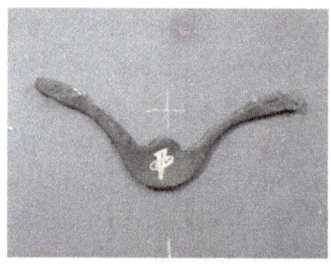

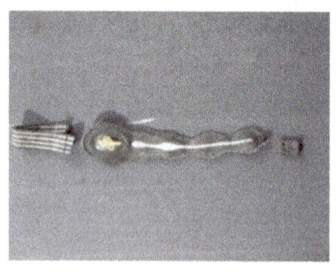

We made changes to all the above stated pieces let's begin by ironing them flat with just enough heat and pressure to avoid stretching the material further. All the stated pieces can be transferred to pattern paper by tracing them except the UPPER its pattern will be created with clear plastic. No need to make a right and left for stated pieces you'll be able to flip them over when there done.

Pattern Pieces

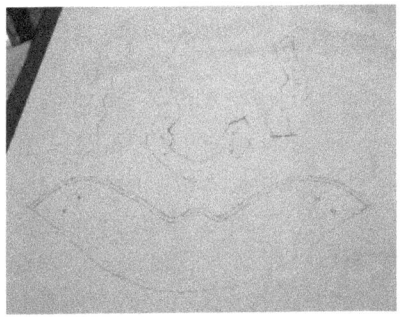

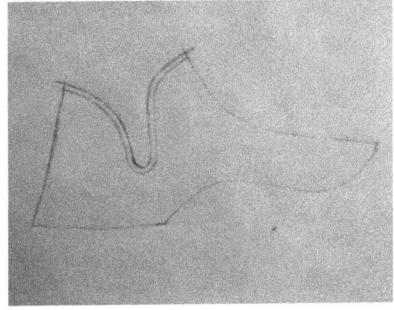

CUSTOMIZED FOAMS

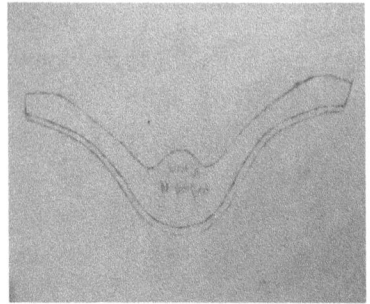

Using clear lightweight plastic cut 2 pieces big enough to cover the sneaker from center back to center front and wide enough to cover it from top to bottom. Using the same kind of plastic cut pieces wide enough to cover the toe box. Now lightly spray some

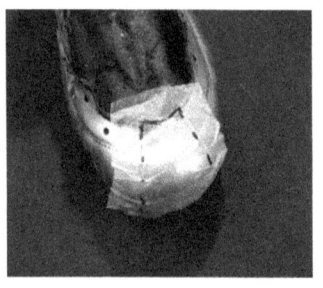

Adhesive on the toe box piece and place it on the toe box area. Begin to trace the seams lines of the toe box all the way around.

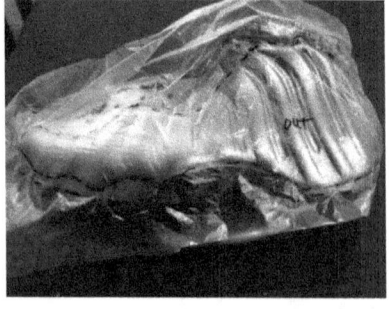

Then re spray and place it on some pattern paper to make further adjustments. (Which we will discuss later). Repeat this process with the inner and outer

portions of the upper. Be sure when aping the plastic you work from one end to the other to ensure a nice flat seal to trace the seams.

Now place all your traced patterns on some pattern paper to strengthen the pattern as well as to make further adjustments. These adjustments are to ensure that certain parts are over lapped and fit properly such as the lace holes and grip areas. **Adjustment 1** add .25" to the top portion of the upper and do the same on the bottom where the grip meets the upper. **Adjustment 2** add .25" to both sides of the toe box pattern and make the top of it flush with the inner and outer upper.

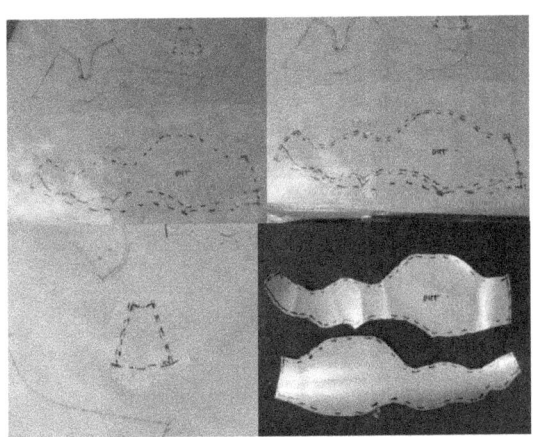

CUSTOMIZED FOAMS

Adjustment 3 we will be adding .50" to the inner liner (lycra) pattern but 1ˢᵗ lets create it by using the outer liner pattern (spacer fabric).

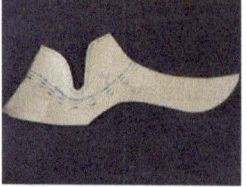

Trace the top portion at the ankle down pass the center scoop a ½" draw a curved lined from one end to another then add the .50" to that line. Double seam allowance to make up for the material lost on the inner liner that will be cut away to replace the top portion of it.

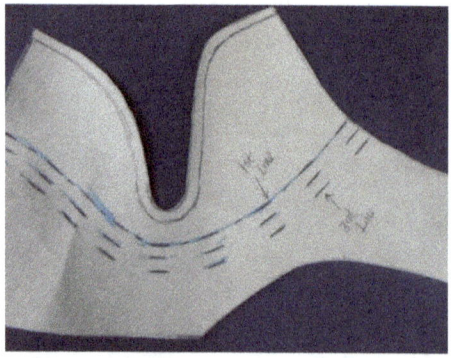

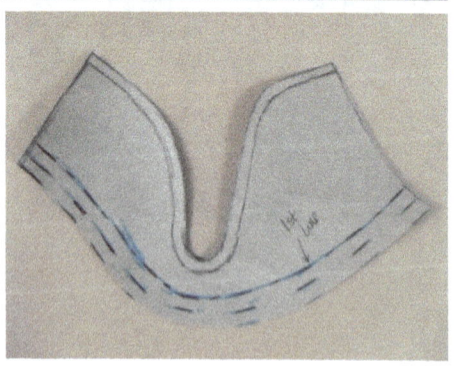

Cut out the patterns you made and prepare to transfer them to the fabric of your choice. But before doing so I would recommend using a mock version of the upper to check the fit of the pattern. It needs to fit nice and tight if it does simply bust the seams and use it as your final pattern.

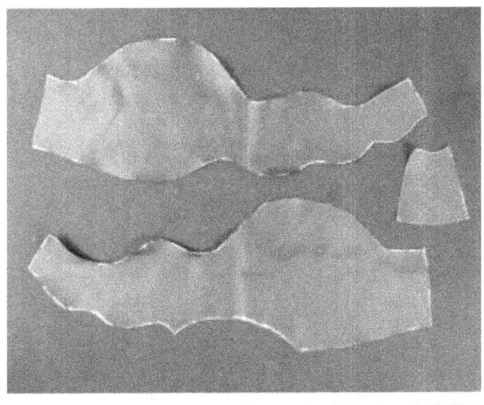

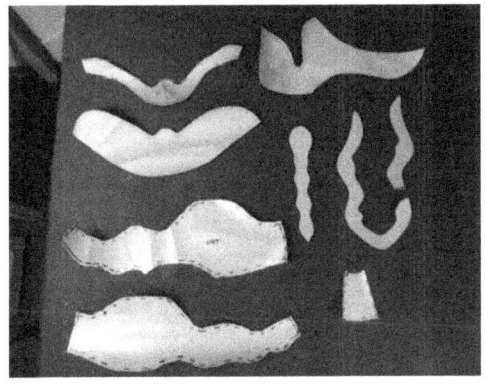

Reconstruction Prep

Here we will be sewing and re-making any whole pieces needed such as the inner and outer uppers the toe box the tongue tabs & decals the inner and outer liner and add the interfacing back to the lace holes as well as adding new cushion (foam) to the inner and outer ankle cushions. You'll need the following tools to complete these task.

TOOLS: Straight Stitch or Zig Zag Sewing Machine, Adhesive Spray, Foam

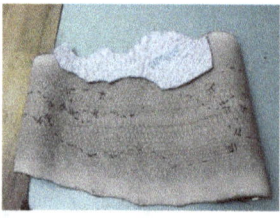

Let's begin by sewing the inner and outer upper and toe box together using the straight stitch machine be sure only to stitch the same allowance you allowed which was the .25" now

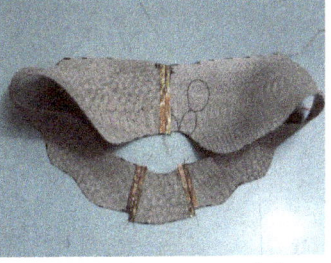

flatten the seams by using a small amount of glue to help with the process.

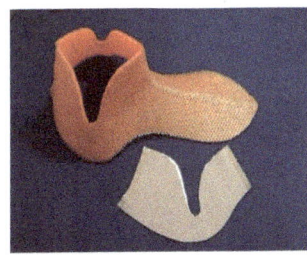

Zig Zag stitch down the front and back of the outer liner (spacer fabric) using the straight stitch or Zig Zag machine. Straight stitch the inner liner (lycra) down the front and back.

Now connect the two together the inner & outer liner (spacer fabric & lycra) around the top only. Reapply adhesive on seams area only flatten and shape in place.

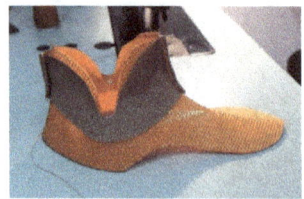

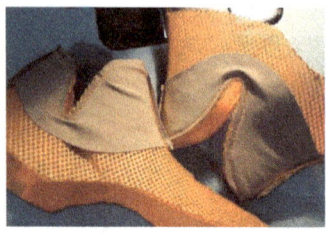

Using the straight the stitch machine sew the logos in place on the tongue decal and outer ankle cushion now tack stitch the pull tabs in place. Now sew the two small tongue decals to the sides of the larger one. Let's finish this up by sewing the completed tongue decal to the outer liner (spacer fabric) making sure not to stitch it to the inner liner (lycra). Use a little glue around the seam edge to flatten the seam put it on the spacer side only and fold over.

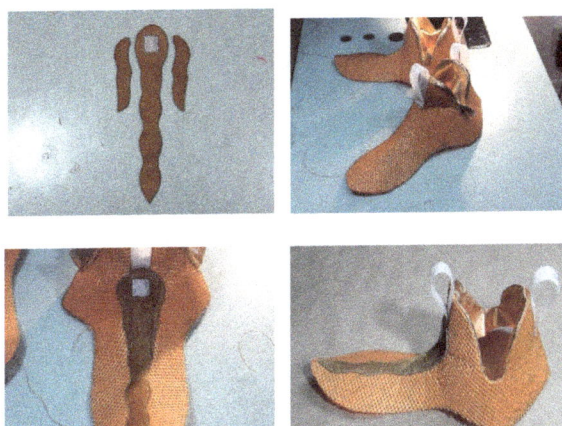

Spray Adhesive on the back of your new inner and outer ankle cushions pieces place them on your new foam then cut them out. This process will ensure that the edges are even all the way around. Use some glue on the bottom edge of the outer ankle cushions and fold over if you intend to glue instead of sewing if your sewing proceed to the next step.

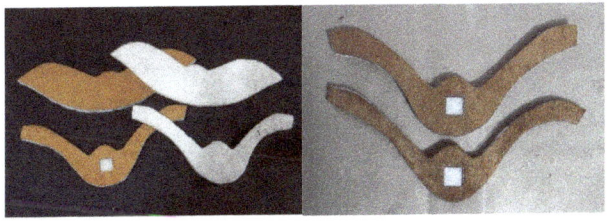

CUSTOMIZED FOAMS

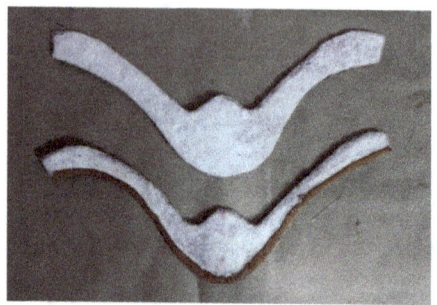

Straight stitch the inside arm of the lace holes bust the seams. Spray adhesive also on the up side of the lace holes interfacing and place them on the back of the lace holes piece be sure to center it.

 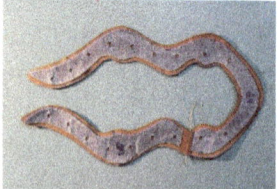

Sneaker Reconstruction

For this portion of production we'll be using the Patchwork Sewing Machine the cylinder arm will allow you to reach every part of the sneaker that needs stitching.

Apply spray adhesive or rubber cement to the inner and outer upper keep the adhesive within the lace holes and grips lightly coated. Flip the upper ½ way inside out so you can place the seam of the upper

against the seams of the sneaker in the back perfectly. Now pull the rest of the skin over the sneaker at the toe box till it's positioned as desired.

CUSTOMIZED FOAMS

Allow 1 to 2 hours to dry before moving to the next step.

ANAGHE INC.

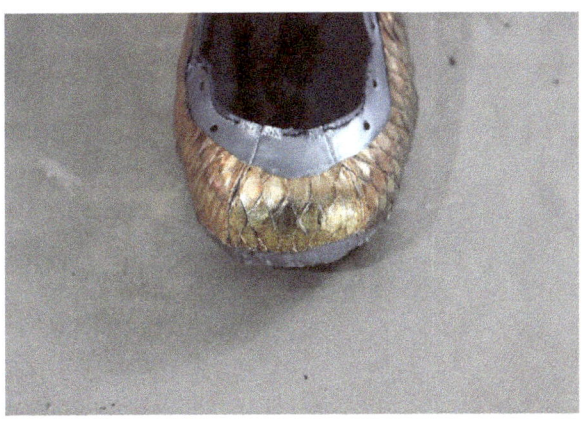

CUSTOMIZED FOAMS

Outside Ankle Cushion Sewing

Let's begin by sewing the outside ankle cushion in place keep in mind it must be sewn up side down then flipped in place. Once sewn apply a small amount of adhesive to the back and fasten it in place. Now there are a few key rules to keep in mind with step. If the material has no stretch you won't be able to use the Patchwork machine to sew it. You'll have to use a Post bed with a roller foot to complete this process.

Outside Ankle Cushion Gluing

Run some glue along the bottom edge of the outside ankle cushion and then turn the edge up .25in hold it in place till a bond is formed. Now run a glue line along where you would 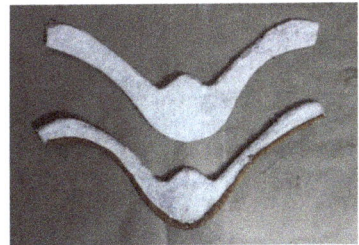 normally stitch the piece in place then fill in the upper portion lightly. Allow the glue to become very tacky apply some to the ankle cushion itself, allow the glue to become tacky. Then center the cushion with the heel seam and press firmly you may have to hold it in place till a bond is formed.

Apply adhesive to the back of the lace holes starting at the toe begin to position the part in place allow 1 to 2 hours to dry before moving to the next step. Now that you positioned the laced holes and dried the allotted time you can begin to stitch it in place using the patchwork sewing machine.

CUSTOMIZED FOAMS

Using the Patchwork machine start sewing the outside portion of the lace holes just make sure you

start in the top corner tip of the part and go tip to corner tip (outside).

For the inside portion you'll need a strip of the 4 way stretch you used to replace the inner liner. Cut it ½" wide and as long as need to reach around the inner lace piece with enough ease on both ends. You will be applying 2 stitch lines to secure the 4 way in place. For the 1st stitch start at the upper portion of the lace holes part and sew along the edge trimming the lace holes with the nylon. The fabric finished sides should be facing each other, the side that will show.

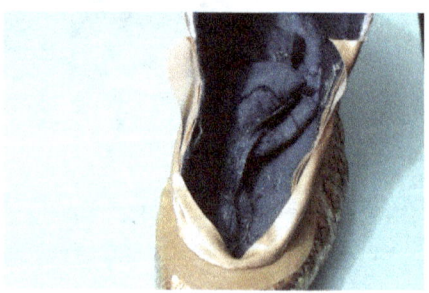

Now before you pull the 4 way nylon over the edge and place stitches along the edge. Cut notches along

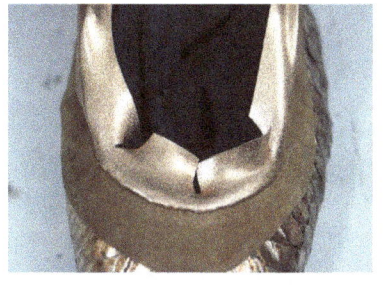

the toe area of the nylon so it fold's under smoothly and remember when placing your stitches get as close as possible to the edge of the nylon. If you can't pull the fabric over and sew at the same time tack glue it in place before sewing it or you can surely glue it. Cut away the excess fabric and prepare to connect the inner ankle cushion.

We extended the length of the 4 way to reach the inner ankle cushion so we will be lining up that part with the center back to find a starting point, sew from one end to the other. Before applying adhesive around the seam cut away the excess fabric from the inner cushion seam side only now turn it over into the heel area then begin to flatten and shape the seam being careful not to dirty your outer liner.

CUSTOMIZED FOAMS

Now we will begin with the reconstruction of the inner and outer liner (spacer/lycra). Using the inner and outer liner pattern mark off a cut line on the sneaker cut on the line.

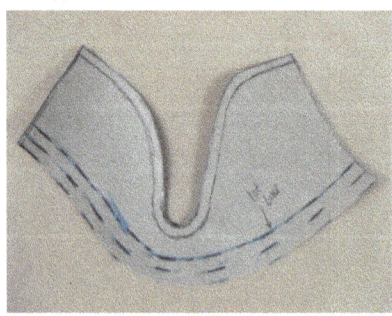

ANAGHE INC.

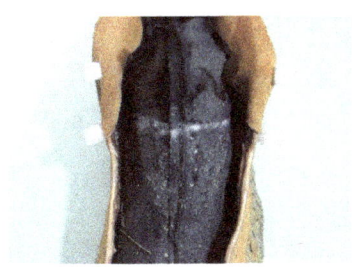

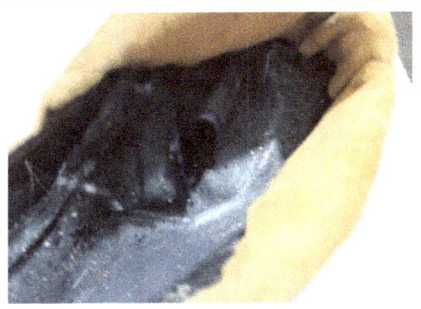

Attach the new inner and outer to the sneaker using the patchwork machine or by hand using a curved needle and a combination of stitches. The 1st the back stitch and then the 2nd is the whip stitch if you would like to cover your frayed ends and add a little more strength to the seam. The back stitch is sufficient on its own and seeing that the area will be covered by the outer liner (spacer) once glue, the whip stitch my not be needed at all. So make sure the seams are facing toward you so they can be covered by the outer liner (spacer).

You will need to cover the cushion area with plastic to keep it clean when flipping the outer liner in place. Now apply adhesive to the under portion of the outer liner (spacer) heavier in the heel area begin to tack it to the inner liner and stitch from one end to the next keep in mind you won't be able to stitch the heel area at all.

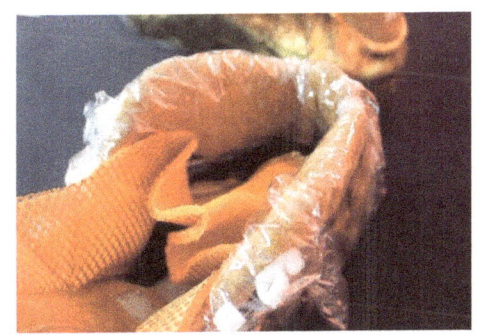

CUSTOMIZED FOAMS

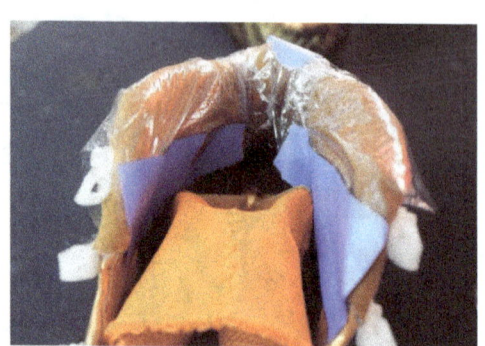

Grip Back On

For reattaching the grip, you're going to need the following tools: RUBBER CEMENT, ELASTIC BANDS, HAND CLAMPS, AND A PAIR OF CALF-HIGH SOCKS (LOL, YEAH A PAIR OF SOCKS) (brand new because you're going to need the tightness of the knit).

Make sure the area you are applying rubber cement to is free of dirt. You're going to be applying at least three coats to the inner part of the grip and to the bottom of  the sneaker on the last. Allow both time to become very tacky before joining them together. Keep in mind to align the center front and the center back of the lasted sneaker and the center front and the center back of the grip before joining them.

Once joined, pressure needs to be applied. Usually in this case a soling machine would be used to create

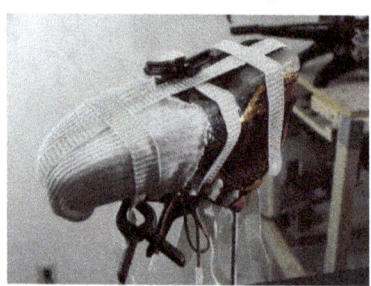

the even pressure needed to join them correctly. I found that elastic bands work well in creating even pressure so spread them out and apply as many as needed to stabilize the grip and lasted sneaker. The Sock Ends create even pressure for the ball of the last, the area on the foot where it bends. You will notice the curve in the last as you attach the grip and how it cuffs at the bend. Your first elastic band will stabilize the center only but not the sides of that area.

Roll the sock up as if you were putting them on and slide them over the sneaker so the double knit surrounds the toe. Begin adding elastic bands to create even more pressure. Allow the sneaker 24 hours to dry before removing the bands. Check where the sneaker and grip meet all the way around for bonding and apply cement to areas that may have not stuck completely.

Then you may have to clean up any loose glue by rolling it away or by brushing it with a suede brush. Remove the sneaker from the last and begin sewing, into the grip if needed. It should be fairly easy because the holes in the sneaker will guide you if lined up properly. The center front and back the holes in the sneaker should line up with the holes in the grip.

Visit us @ www.anaghe.com to preview the finish pair (Fire & Ice) and to watch the step by step instructional videos to increase your learning experience. These videos are available ONLY to Book buyers and Members of Anaghe&Co. And be sure to inquire about our 1 on 1 classes in the members section.

Thank You So Much for this purchase & may God Bless your hands to create the desires of your heart!

CUSTOMIZED FOAMS

ANAGHE INC.

Stitch Classifaction & Instruction

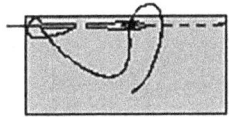

Secure the thread with tiny back stitches at the beginning of the work and with a figure-8 knot at the end. For the figure-8 knot, take a tiny back stitch, wrap the thread under and around the needle before pulling the needle through.

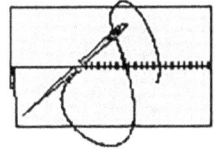

The **fell stitch** is useful for joining two layers of fabric from the right side. Insert the needle directly below where it came out of the fabric, and bring it out 1/8" ahead and opposite where it first came out of the fabric. There will be diagonal stitches on the wrong side.

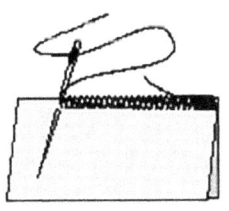

The **whipstitch** is used for seaming fabrics, either right or wrong sides together. The stitches should be about 1/16" apart, and only as deep as necessary to create a firm seam. Leave a tail of thread when you start, and work several stitches over it to secure and hide the thread.

CUSTOMIZED FOAMS

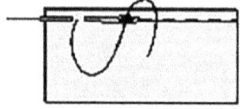

The **backstitch** makes a very strong seam. Take a 1/8" stitch, then insert the needle either 1/16 or 1/8" behind the thread, and take another 1/8" stitch.

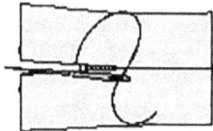

The **drawing stitch** invisibly joins two layers of fabric with folded edges from the right side. Take a short stitch through one folded edge, then in the other folded edge.

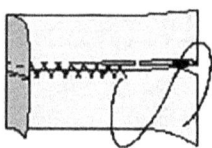

The **catch stitch** is very useful for hemming as well as joining two edges. Take a small backstitch, move to the other layer, and take another backstitch.

REVERSE OXIDATION PROCESS

Most of you are like me we have an old pair of sneakers that have yellowed. Where there used to be white rubber now looks like peed on snow. In some sneakers in may add character, but in others ….not so much. Maybe if there was some sort of way to undo this. Being able to breathe more life and add value back in a pair of Jordan's. Which makes the difference at market on the price tag. What we intend to cover in this bonus section is the standard practice for removing the yellowing. BE ADVISED this is long process! The whole thing should take a week max; if not there are issues in the process. The process in which the rubber yellowing is called reverse oxidation. It's caused by exposure to the sun and all of its ultra violet rays. Ironic enough ultra violet rays are needed to reverse it.

REFLECTIVE BOX AND LIGHT

A reflective box is just any box big enough to sit the soles in. That is lined with aluminum foil. Now the light is an Anaghe T5 Oxidation Light it has 10,000 lumens with a blue white color spectrum. Hang it a least 1ft away from the reflective box. This is a long process so keep that in mind when selecting a location for the light. It has to run for 10 to 14 hours a day so you may want to use a closet or an empty room. Depending on the time you have it's possible to space out the sessions. You need a total of 6 days which equals to 50 to 84 hours of light.

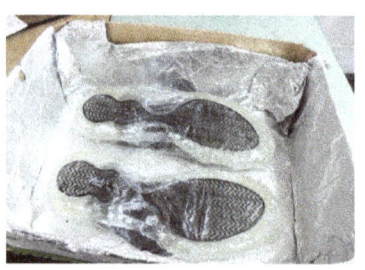

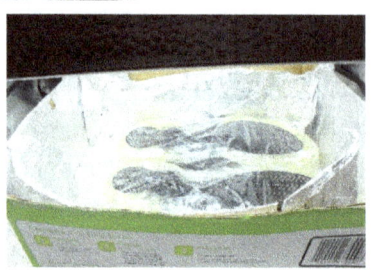

APPLY WHITENER

Now there are many sneaker sole whiteners on the market some work better than others and you may have a product that works for you but we found mixing them together you can achieve even better results. Clean the sole up remove any glue wash them with soap and water dry them completely. Apply your sauce to the yellowed sole portion please remember to wear gloves because THIS STUFF BURNS. They all burn WEAR GLOVES!!!

CUSTOMIZED FOAMS

WRAP SHOES

Wrap your shoes using household cling wrap. The purpose of this is to keep the sauce moist throughout the time under the light. If it dries that means the peroxide has evaporated apply more sauce when this happens. Place the soles in the reflective box and hang the light a least 1ft away but with the Anaghe T5 Oxidation Light you don't have to worry about the grip smoothing out due to heat, so cut outs are no longer needed.

2 Sessions 2 Days 28 Hours of Light

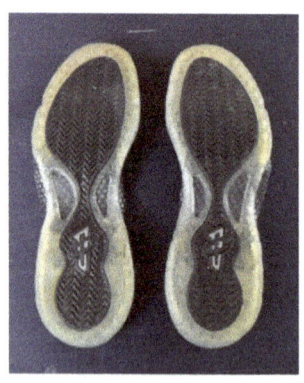 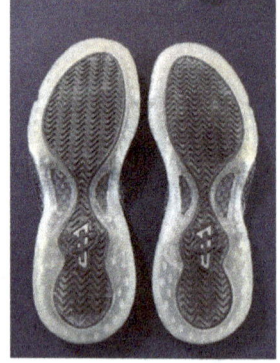

ANAGHE INC.

4 Sessions 4 Days 56 Hours of Light

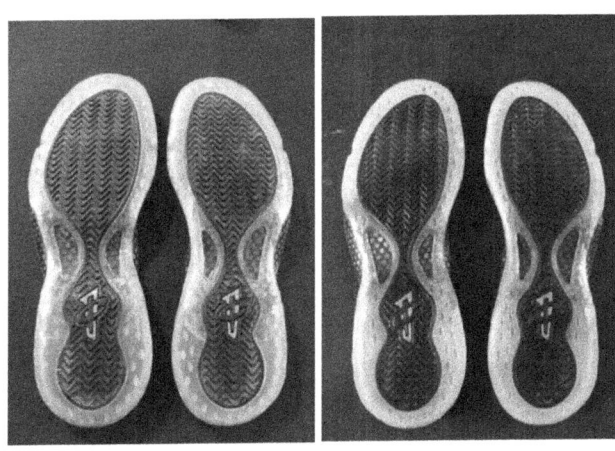

www.ingramcontent.com/pod-product-compliance
Lightning Source LLC
Chambersburg PA
CBHW070552300426
44113CB00011B/1886